Grammar and Punctuation

ACTIVITY BOOK

Written by
Rhona Whiteford and Jim Fitzsimmons

Illustrated by Natascha Nazarova

CONTENTS

Ladybird

Sentences make sense

A **sentence** is a group of words that makes sense on its own.
A sentence always contains a **verb** or "doing word".
It always begins with a capital letter and ends with

• a full stop, **?** a question mark or **!** an exclamation mark.

1 Complete these sentences by joining the two halves that make sense together.

The truck	was fast asleep.
The builder	kept fine all day.
The field	parked at the side of the road.
The weather	was green and level.

2 Write this passage out again, adding capital letters and full stops to make sentences.

you cannot build a house without a plan it would be a disaster if you did imagine how many mistakes could be made building is a skilled business

How many sentences did you write? ☐

Different kinds of sentences

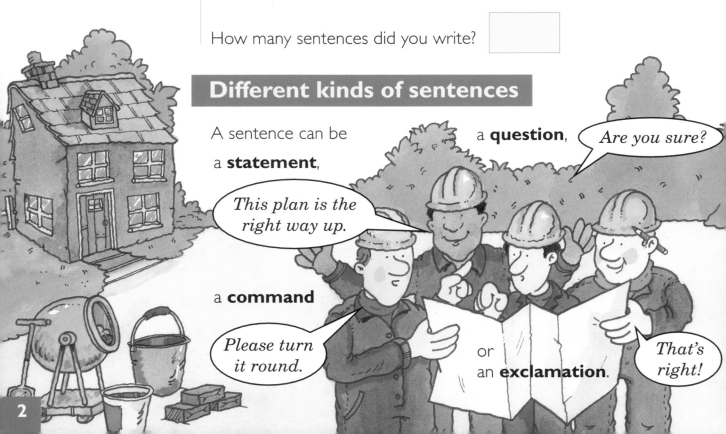

A sentence can be a **statement**, a **question**,

Are you sure?

This plan is the right way up.

a **command**

Please turn it round.

or an **exclamation**.

That's right!

3 Put an **S**, **Q**, **C** or **E**, for **s**tatement, **q**uestion, **c**ommand or **e**xclamation, on Sam's hard hat or above the foreman's head to show what kind of sentence is being said.

Breaking down sentences

To understand how sentences work, it helps to break them down into their different parts. A sentence can be divided into two parts.

The **subject** tells us who or what the sentence is about.

The **predicate** tells us what is said or written about the subject.

| The carpenter | cuts the wood. |

| It | is expensive wood. |

4 Draw brackets round the subject and underline the predicate in these sentences.

> The plumber picked up a piece of pipe.
>
> The pipe was not long enough.
>
> Someone had made a mistake.

5 The subject doesn't always come at the beginning of a sentence. Find the subject of these sentences.

> Does your dog bark?
>
> Sometimes it barks in the middle of the night.
>
> How do you manage to sleep?

Sentence sense...

Sometimes a command or exclamation misses out the subject when it is "you" because everyone knows who or what is meant.

You name it – nouns

A **noun** is a word that names someone or something.

> *I am a* *builder* .

1 Draw a ring round the words that are nouns.

> house plan was hopeful idea music happily hedge
> hello Charlotte girl team friendly enemy decide
> plumber pretty Africa fright afraid longest diver

Different kinds of nouns

Proper nouns start with a capital letter. They name one particular person or place or thing.

> *Jo , Bob , Sheena and Sam are going to play for the All Stars in Newtown .*

Common nouns name things in a more general way. Usually the same noun can be used to name lots of similar things.

> *But here are their* *shirts* , *shorts and trainers* !

> *I've an* *idea* *that their* *forgetfulness will cause* *panic* .

Abstract nouns name things that cannot be seen, touched, tasted, heard or smelt, such as feelings or ideas.

> *It would take an* *army* *to keep that* *team* *in order!*

Collective nouns name a group or collection of people or things.

2 Write the nouns on the pile of bricks in the correct places to fill the gaps in the wall.

Proper nouns	Anna				
Common nouns	wall				
Abstract nouns	success				
Collective nouns	crowd				

Sita anger hope Tuesday brain dream Thames Johnson
brick tree herd cement bunch swarm courage group

Pronouns

Where is my spade ?

I gave it to him !

Who took my hat ?

Pronouns are used in place of **nouns** to avoid repeating them.

Be careful to use pronouns only when it is quite clear who or what you mean.

I you he she it we they

These pronouns are used in place of a noun that is the **subject** of a sentence. The subject tells us who or what the sentence is about.

me you him her it us them

These pronouns are used in place of a noun that is the **object** of a sentence. The object has the action of the verb or "doing word" done to it.

1 On another piece of paper, write out this passage, replacing each underlined noun with a suitable pronoun.

> Sam gave the spade to Sheena. <u>Sheena</u> gave <u>the spade</u> to Bob. <u>Bob</u> lent <u>the spade</u> to Sam. "Where did <u>Bob</u> get <u>the spade</u>? " <u>Sam</u> asked.

Nouns that show possession or belonging can be replaced by **possessive pronouns**.

mine yours his hers its ours theirs

2 Fill in the missing pronouns to answer the questions.

Is that your spade?   Yes, this is . . . .

Is that Sam's hat?   Yes, that is . . . .

Is that our van?   Yes, that <u>was</u> . . . .

Amazing adjectives

What a handsome , clever , *friendly* little *dog!*

Adjectives are words that describe a noun or pronoun.

1 Underline the adjectives in the surveyor's report. How many adjectives did you find?

As well as poor brickwork and four rotting windows, this old house shows some signs of rising damp. New visitors should watch out for falling tiles.

2 Use the adjectives in the list below to fill the gaps in the estate agent's description.

three
delightful
this
some
outstanding
interested

.... house has .... rooms on .... floors. Although it is in need of .... repair, the house should be viewed as soon as possible by all .... buyers.

3 Some adjectives are made from nouns. Make adjectives from the nouns in brackets to fill in the gaps. Use your dictionary to help you.

Sam made a .... mistake. (fool)

He used a .... hammer. (fault)

Suddenly he heard a .... howl. (dread)

"Do have this .... bone," said Sam. (beauty)

Comparative and superlative adjectives

Comparative and **superlative adjectives** are used to compare things.

Adjective	Comparative	Superlative
 big	bigger	biggest

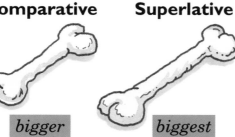

Short adjectives usually add **er** to become comparatives and **est** to become superlatives. Longer adjectives stay the same but the word **more** or **most** is put in front of them. A few adjectives change completely.

4 Fill in the spaces with the correct form of the adjective.

Adjective	Comparative	Superlative
long		
	more careful	
		most handsome
	cleverer	
sad		
good		

5 Choose an adjective from the list below and use the correct form to complete each sentence.

bad
old
difficult

This house is the .... building in the country.

It has the .... case of dry rot I have ever seen.

This will be a .... job than the one we tackled last week.

Adjective advice...

better!

best!

Use a comparative adjective when you are comparing two things and a superlative adjective when you are comparing more than two.

Vital verbs

A **verb** is a **doing** or **being** word.

I like sandwiches.

Come back!

He looks unfit.

I am exhausted.

I love sandwiches.

A verb may be made up of more than one word.

I often run for exercise.

I do run for exercise.

I am running for exercise.

1 Underline the verbs in this passage. Be careful to find all the words that make up the verb.

Exercise is important! We must become more fit. I am taking my health very seriously. You should do the same. Come with me on my early morning run! What do you say?

Tenses

Verbs are used in different **tenses** so that we know whether something happened in the **past**, or is happening now in the **present**, or will happen in the **future**. In some tenses the verb also needs more than one word.

2 Write **past**, **present**, or **future** in the space under each speech bubble to show what kind of verb is being used.

3 Fill in the gaps with verbs to show what happened yesterday and what will happen tomorrow. The verbs will need to be in the past tense and the future tense.

Today I am fit. Yesterday I .... unfit. Tomorrow I .... very fit.

Today I am going to bed early. Yesterday I .... to bed late. Tomorrow I .... to bed even earlier.

What are you doing today? What .... you .... yesterday? What .... you .... tomorrow?

Questions

He is *ready.*

She likes *walking.*

To change a statement into a question, we often put the words in a different order. In the present tense, we sometimes have to change the verb and add an extra word as well to form a question.

We want *to run a marathon.*

Do *we* want *to run a marathon?*

Does *she* like *walking?*

Is *he ready?*

Tenses tip...

A question with a changed verb should still make sense if you turn it back into a statement. "Does she like walking?" would become "She does like walking." That is another way of saying "She likes walking." It is still in the present tense.

4 Write out these sentences again as questions. Decide whether you can just change the order of the words or if you need to change the verb as well.

You are a good worker.
You work hard.
You always do as you are told.
I am paying you enough.
That seems fair.

Verbs and their subjects

All sentences have a **subject** and a **verb**. Verbs sometimes change to suit their subjects.

They work *hard.*

I work *hard.*

He works *hard.*

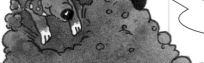

Usually it is the verbs that go with **he**, **she** and **it** that change in the present tense. Watch out for the verb **to be**, which does not follow the same pattern.

Are *you* hungry?

I am !

We are !

She is !

They are !

5 Cross out the wrong forms of the verb **to be** in these sentences.

I is/am/are ready to go home.
You is/am/are tired.
He is/am/are even more tired.
We is/am/are completely exhausted!

Verbs and their objects

Some **verbs** also need an **object**. The object has the action of the verb done to it.

They *have broken* *the window* . *I* *will mend* *it* .

If you take the object away the sentence does not make sense. A verb that needs an object is called a **transitive** verb.

Some verbs do not need objects. They are called **intransitive** verbs. Verbs that are "being words" are always intransitive.

The window *seems* *fine.* *You* *are* *clever.*

"Fine" and "clever" are adjectives and give us more information about the noun or pronoun that is the subject.

6 Draw a ring round the subject, underline the verb and put brackets round the object in these sentences. Be careful! Not all the sentences have objects.

I have been mending windows for many years. I am always very careful. You must wear gloves. The broken glass can cut you badly.

Active adverbs

We must use this cement quickly *and* carefully .

An **adverb** tells us more about a verb. It tells us how, when or where the action of a verb happens.

Many adverbs end in **ly** and can be made from **adjectives**.

1 Complete each pair of sentences by changing the adjectives in the first sentence into adverbs.

You are brave, helpful, quiet and sensible. You work bravely,

. . . .

He is noisy, careless and lazy. He works . . . .

. . . .

Adverbial phrases also tell us how, when or where an action happens.

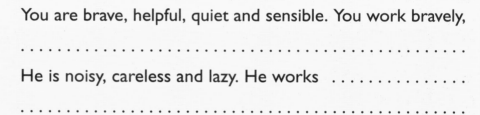

As quickly as you can , *take that cement* over there .

2 After each sentence, write one adverb that could be used to replace the underlined adverbial phrase.

They moved the cement <u>with care</u>. . . . .

They dropped a little bit <u>by accident</u>. . . . .

Then they had to hide <u>in a hurry</u>. . . . .

The foreman was spluttering <u>in fury</u>. . . . .

3 Underline the adverbial phrases and put a ring round the adverbs in the reference that the foreman wrote for Bob.

Bob works well most of the time. He moves quickly when necessary and always works cheerfully. Sometimes he does not listen properly but he willingly corrects all his mistakes.

How many adverbs did you find?

How many adverbial phrases were there?

4 Write out this rather boring newspaper report again, replacing the gaps with your own choice of adverbs or adverbial phrases. Try to make the story as exciting as possible and add a sentence to clear up the mystery of the white shape.

... (when?) ... the watchman on the building site woke up ... (how?) ... Someone was moving ... (how?) ... outside his window. "I waited ... (how long?) ...," explained Mr. Guard ... (how?) ..., "and ...(when?) ... decided to go outside. I ran ... (where?) ... and saw a white shape that moved ... (how?) ... (when?) ... I went back inside."

5 Put a ring round the adverbs and a line under the adjectives. If you are not sure, try each word in a sentence.

steadily   steady   happily   contented   musical

tunefully   hard   easy   easily

Which word from the list above can you use as both an adjective and an adverb?

Conjunctions join up

A **compound** sentence is made of two or more simple sentences joined together by a joining word called a **conjunction** .

The weather is very bad. We cannot work.

The weather is very bad and *we cannot work.*

1 Copy these sentences, using a conjunction from the list below to join each pair together.

| but | and | for |
| so | yet | or |

2 Underline the clauses and put a ring round the phrases.

3 On a separate piece of paper, write out the phrases and clauses in exercise **2** to form a sentence. Remember to begin with a capital letter and end with a full stop. Use commas to separate each clause and phrase.

My shoes are wet. My hair is wet.
My feet are wet. My hair is dry.
It might go on raining. It might stop raining.
I think it will stop. The sky is clearing.
It is clearing over there. The rain is still heavy.

Complex sentences are made up of **clauses** and **phrases**.

A **phrase** is a group of words that does not make complete sense on its own and does not contain a verb.

A **clause** is a group of words that does contain a verb or "doing word".

grumbling to themselves

inside the leaky hut

bored and hungry

the builders were huddling

Clause clue...

The most important clause in a sentence is called the **main clause**. If it is taken away, the sentence does not make sense. The main clause **does** make sense by itself. It is like a little sentence hidden inside a longer sentence.

Clauses can be joined by **conjunctions**. The conjunction does not have to come between the clauses it is joining.

If the rain stops soon, we can finish the roof.

I am staying right here *until* the rain stops.

We will be late finishing *because* the weather is so bad.

As the weather is so bad, no one will expect us to finish early.

4 Choose conjunctions from the list below to complete the passage.

if while as
until though
because
although since
unless where
whenever
wherever

Foreman's Report

.... the weather has been very poor, good progress has been made. .... we have no more rain, we shall finish on time. There will be no more problems .... the sun keeps shining. We cannot work under shelter .... the roof is not yet on.

Commas

Later today, if the weather stays fine, we will finish the roof.

, are used to make brief pauses in a sentence.

When a sentence has several phrases and clauses, commas are placed between them to make the sentence clearer and easier to read.

1 Put commas between the phrases and clauses in these sentences so that they are easier to read.

> Before the end of the day someone must count the tiles. As soon as the roof is finished the carpenters can start work inside. If everyone works hard without making any silly mistakes the job will soon be done.

Commas are also used to separate items in a list. In a simple list, a comma is put after each item except the last two, which are joined with a **conjunction**, such as **and** or **or**.

Sam, Jim, Ali, Myra and Jacky are working on the roof.

2 Finish these sentences by adding three items from the list below.

The builders need . . . .

tiles
nails
roofing felt
chocolates
toffees
mints
garage
supermarket
store

. . . . are the foreman's favourite sweets.

Shall I go to the . . . . first?

Looking at lists...

If a list is a complicated one, where there are conjunctions as part of the list, commas are used to separate **all** the items in the list, including the last one, to avoid confusion.

I like blue and yellow, red and green, and pink and orange wallpaper.

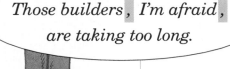

Those builders, I'm afraid, are taking too long.

Commas can also be used in pairs to separate a phrase or clause from the rest of the sentence. The sentence still makes sense if the part inside the commas is taken away.

Remember, when you are using commas in this way, that you need one **before** the phrase or clause and one **after** it.

3 Use pairs of commas to separate the phrase or clause in the middle of each of these sentences.

> Everyone will you know have to work faster.
> Where do you think are the two missing workers?
> You can have a rest Jim and Ali when I say so.
> Now the work will I hope go more smoothly.

4 Write out this passage again, putting in all the capital letters, full stops and commas needed.

> it will soon be time I think to paint the doors windows and fence if possible I shall use all the colours of the rainbow those are if I remember correctly red orange yellow green blue indigo and violet it is possible I suppose that the result would be <u>too</u> bright

How many commas did you use?

with singular nouns
with plural nouns
replacing letters

Apostrophes

Does this car belong to Myra?

, An **apostrophe** is used to show possession. It shows who or what something belongs to.

Yes, this is Myra's car.

If it is a singular noun doing the possessing, the apostrophe comes after the noun and is followed by an **s**.

1 Answer the questions using an apostrophe.

Does this hat belong to Sam? Yes, that is .... hat.

Does this spade belong to a builder? Yes, that is a

.... spade.

Is this the house where Jess lives? Yes, this is .... house.

If it is a plural noun doing the possessing, the apostrophe also comes after the noun. If the plural noun does **not** already end with an **s**, an **s** is added **after** the apostrophe.

The builders' boots are muddier than the children's shoes.

2 Complete each sentence using an apostrophe.

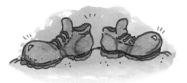

These boots belong to the builders.

They are the .... boots.

The children have lost their ball.

Here is the .... ball.

These cars belong to those women.

They are the .... cars.

3 Something always seems to be missing on a building site! Add an apostrophe and an **s** if necessary to each of the items on the foreman's list.

Sam.... second-best spade   the carpenters.... biggest nails

an electrician.... screwdriver   all the builders.... lunches

Punctuation point...

Unlike the nouns they replace, possessive pronouns, such as **yours**, **hers**, **theirs** and **ours**, do not have apostrophes.

Missing letters

An apostrophe is also used to show where a word has been shortened by missing out letters.

I am sleepy this morning.   *I'm sleepy too!*

4 Use one of the shortened words in the bag to fill each gap. Don't forget that sentences must start with a capital letter.

you've   I've
he's   don't
you're

You have made a mess. .... made a terrible mess!

You are careless. .... really careless!

I do not know what to do with you. I just .... know!

He is more untidy than you. .... even more untidy!

I have warned you before. .... warned you!

5 Write these words out in full.

can't . . . .   wouldn't . . . .

I've   . . . .   hasn't . . . .

isn't   . . . .   where's . . . .

Be careful with **its** and **it's**. **Its** is a possessive pronoun that does not have an apostrophe. **It's** is short for **it is** and does have an apostrophe.

6 Cross out the wrong word in each sentence.

Its/It's a beautiful day today. I've cleaned my car and washed its/it's windows. Its/it's paintwork is so shiny, its/it's dazzling. Oh no! Its/It's starting to rain!

Inverted commas

Inverted commas (quotation marks) are used to show the words that someone actually says. This is called **direct speech**.

" **Opening inverted commas** are used **before** the words actually said.

" **Closing inverted commas** are used **after** the words actually said.

Remember that opening and closing inverted commas **always** work together in pairs, at each end of the direct speech.

It is time for lunch.

The foreman said, "It is time for lunch."

We put a **comma** between the words that introduce the foreman's speech and what he actually said. The comma comes **before** the opening inverted commas.

I Finish these sentences to show what was said. Remember to write all the speech, including its punctuation.

I hate egg rolls.	Sam said, ...
Why is that?	Myra asked, ...
I don't know.	Sam replied, ...
You are funny, Sam!	Myra exclaimed, ...
	....

If a speech in inverted commas ends in the middle of a larger sentence, the full stop at the end of the speech is changed into a **comma** (inside the closing inverted commas). If a speech ends with a **question mark** or **exclamation mark**, these are not changed when they come in the middle of a larger sentence.

"Why is that?" asked Myra.   *"I don't know," replied Sam.*

2 Write the sentences in exercise **1** again with the speech in inverted commas coming at the beginning of each sentence.

.... said Sam.

.... Myra asked.

.... Sam replied.

.... Myra exclaimed.

If a speech in inverted commas is **interrupted** in a sentence, each part of the speech should have opening and closing inverted commas.

A **comma** inside the closing inverted commas separates the first part of the speech from the words that interrupt it.

The interrupting words are also separated from the next part of the speech by a comma.

"In fact," said Myra, "you are the funniest person I know!"

*"Do you mean," asked Sam, "that you **do** like egg rolls?"*

3 Write out these sentences on a piece of paper, changing them round so that they are interrupted where you see the space.

"How nice it is   to eat outdoors," said Sam.
"If only   there were no insects!" cried Myra.
"The insects   are not bothering me," Sam replied.
"Perhaps   they don't like egg rolls either!" laughed Myra.

Organising your writing

A **paragraph** is a group of sentences about the same subject. When you are doing a long piece of writing, it is a good idea to start a new paragraph when you mention a new idea or event.

Once upon a time there was a very silly king, who wanted to have an adventure. Nothing exciting ever happened to him.

One day a stranger came to the palace. He wore black from head to foot and carried...

Usually the first line of a new paragraph starts a little further to the right than the rest of the writing.

Here a new paragraph has been started because a new character has come into the story.

1 Write out these instructions as three paragraphs.

Before you begin to paint a door, you should make sure the surface is clean and smooth. Use sandpaper on any rough spots. Do not paint on a very windy day or when it may rain. Choose a warm, still day. Open the tin of paint carefully and stir it thoroughly before you begin work.

MY HOLIDAY
- The journey
- The campsite
- Sam's adventure
- How we decided to go to Spain
- My holiday memories

2 The foreman has made some notes about the report he has to make to his boss. Write a number from 1 to 6 in the boxes to show the correct order for his report.

If you have a lot to say or a long story to tell, it is a good idea to make short notes about what you will write about in each paragraph. Looking at your notes will help you to decide whether you have put your ideas in the best order. It is easier to change your plan now than when you are halfway through your writing.

☐ Surveying the site

☐ Putting the roof on

☐ Digging the foundations

☐ Building the walls

☐ Painting and decorating

☐ Leaving the site

Writing letters

There is a special way to set out a letter so that it is clear and easy to read for the person who receives it.

Write the date under your address.

Write your own address at the top right of the page. Put commas at the end of each line and a full stop at the end of the address. The postcode has no punctuation.

Builder's Rest,
12, New Road,
Newtown,
Midshire.
MI99 9AB

1st August 1995

Dear Sam,

Put a comma after the name of the person you are writing to. If the person is not a close friend, write   Dear Mr. Davies,
            Dear Mrs. Davies,
            Dear Miss Davies,
or   Dear Ms. Davies,

If you do not know the person's name, write
            Dear Sir,
or   Dear Madam,

While you were on holiday, we finished work on the house. We are all going to meet on the site for a celebration picnic at lunchtime next Wednesday.
    Please come. We all look forward to seeing you.

            Yours,

            Myra

P.S. Please bring something to eat!

Leave a margin on both sides of the writing and at the top and bottom of the page.

Put a comma after the ending of the letter. If the letter is to a friend, you could put Love, or Best wishes,

If the letter is to a person who is not a close friend, you could put Yours sincerely,

You can add a last-minute thought to a friend by putting the initials P.S.

If the letter is to someone whose name you don't know, you should put Yours faithfully,

3 Write your address on this envelope. Set it out just as you would at the top of a letter, but position it in the middle of the envelope.

4 Write another letter from Myra to Sam on a separate piece of paper, explaining that the picnic is still taking place but will be on Thursday, not Wednesday.

Well done! Fill in the certificate to show that you have completed this book.

Certificate

This is to certify that

_____

of

_____

_____

_____

_____

has successfully completed the activities in the
Grammar and Punctuation activity book

Date: _____   Signed: _____

Parent/Teacher/Carer